Inside the Mind of

Kim Kardashian

The Brain Institute for Studies on Intelligence

Printed in Great Britain
by Amazon

34649584R00116